THE ENTREPRENEUR'S
FOUNDATION FOR SUCCESS
BUSINESS GROWTH

FIRST THIS, THEN THAT

Companion Workbook

LESLIE HASSLER

STRATEGIX
PRESS

Dallas, Texas

COMPANION WORKBOOK FOR
Your Biz Rules Guide

FIRST THIS, THEN THAT
THE ENTREPRENEUR'S FOUNDATION FOR SUCCESSFUL BUSINESS GROWTH

LESLIE HASSLER

Published by:

STRATEGIX PRESS

Strategix Press
16206 Spring Creek Rd, Dallas, TX 75248

ISBN: 979-8-9904475-6-1

CONTENTS

WELCOME
TO THE COMPANION WORKBOOK

This workbook is designed to compliment the book *First This, Then That* written by Leslie Hassler.

It takes the practical teachings and puts them in a workbook format to help you experience the transformation in your business.

We hope you enjoy both books!

If you have not bought *First This, Then That*, head to
https://www.yourbizrules.com/buyfttt/

Chapter 1

Your Business, Your Rules
Navigating the Road
to Strategic Success

Have you had a time period that made you doubt your business? If so, what is it? If not, what is your biggest fear in/for your business?

What are you telling yourself that needs a mindset adjustment?

How can you reword those phrases into positive statements?

On the next page, I want you to dream about your business. Use the prompts provided to describe things you would change. Please note that this is a judgement-free zone where you can dream of anything! The more descriptive you can be, the better. Use this time to claim the business you want to have.

What does "Heaven" look like in your business?

How would your clients show up? How would they behave? Who would they be?

How would your team show up? How would they feel? Who would they be?

What impact would you have on clients, community & your team?

Where would the revenue be for positive fiscal health? What would that mean?

How would you feel as the owner? Who would you need to be to make this happen?

What is the Vision of Your Business?

Pick a time 1-3 years or more to dream about what your business can be. Be as descriptive as you can.

Today's date _____________

The date _______ year(s) from now will be _____________

This is your time. Claim it.

What is the Vision of Your Business?

Based on the vision you've set for your business, take a moment to reflect on these questions.

Where are you or have been settling in your business? Are there any results you wish you had in your business that you don't currently have?

Why is it important to reach this vision? What will it mean for you and your life?

Why is this vision worth protecting?

Notes

Notes

Notes

Chapter 2

Master Your Finances
Beyond Vanity Metrics
to Sustainable Profit

How do you feel about money? (Uneasy—perhaps causing your stomach to churn, your blood pressure to rise, or making you feel slightly offended) OR (feeling comfortable, relaxed, calm, and at ease.)

What is the earliest memory of that feeling?

Take a minute and consider your first memory of hearing others talk about money. What was said at that time? If you could go back in time, what would you share about the experience with your younger self?

How Is The Cash In Your Business Behaving?

Rate your business performance on the three categories of money management to understand where your opportunities for improvement lie.

MONEY IN

Profitable Pricing	1 2 3 4 5 6 7 8 9 10
Pipeline Development	1 2 3 4 5 6 7 8 9 10
Revenue Layering	1 2 3 4 5 6 7 8 9 10
Account Receivables	1 2 3 4 5 6 7 8 9 10

MONEY STEWARDSHIP

Predictive Cash Flow	1 2 3 4 5 6 7 8 9 10
Culture of Results	1 2 3 4 5 6 7 8 9 10
Building Leverage	1 2 3 4 5 6 7 8 9 10
Taking Profit First	1 2 3 4 5 6 7 8 9 10

MONEY OUT

Money Leak Management	1 2 3 4 5 6 7 8 9 10
Expense Management	1 2 3 4 5 6 7 8 9 10
Feedback Loops	1 2 3 4 5 6 7 8 9 10
Fiscal Responsibility	1 2 3 4 5 6 7 8 9 10

Money Traps

Score Yourself on the Money Traps You Fall Into:

Rarely <-----> Often

Trap #1:
Find Your Passion and
the Money Will Follow

Score 1 2 3 4 5

Trap #2:
Skipping the Math

Score 1 2 3 4 5

Trap #3:
Hard Work Gets
Rewarded

Score 1 2 3 4 5

Trap #4:
Managing Your Money
on a Hope and Prayer

Score 1 2 3 4 5

Trap #5:
If I Grow, I Will Solve
My Cash Problems

Score 1 2 3 4 5

Which money trap did you score the highest/most often?

What do you need to do to change that?

What are your profit expectations?

If you're merely breaking even, when do you expect to become genuinely profitable?

What's your magic number where you become profitable?

Notes

Notes

Notes

Chapter 3

Predictable Profits
Cash Flow Systems That Work

Which animal personifies how you handle your money?

OSTRICH

Do you put your head in the sand and trust that your money is fine? (Maybe someone else looks at it?)

RHINO

Do you find yourself charging in to make decisions very reactionary?

OWL

Do you look at your money strategically to put a plan in place and make wise decisions?

What would it take for you to become aware of your money like an owl?

Your Power P&L Numbers

Get your Profit & Loss Statement and let's use your power numbers to do some quick calculations. Note: If you do not know how to get your P&L, that is step 1 on becoming an owl. You got this!

<table>
<tr><td colspan="3">Profit & Loss</td></tr>
<tr><td>Income</td><td></td><td></td></tr>
<tr><td></td><td>40100 - Construction Income</td><td>$ 65,447.32</td></tr>
<tr><td></td><td>40500 - Reimbursement Income</td><td>$ 461.81</td></tr>
<tr><td>1</td><td>Total Income</td><td>$ 65,909.16</td></tr>
<tr><td>Cost of Good Sold</td><td></td><td></td></tr>
<tr><td></td><td>50100 - Cost of Goods Sold</td><td>$ 1,197.48</td></tr>
<tr><td></td><td>5400 - Job Expenses</td><td>$ 24,758.30</td></tr>
<tr><td></td><td>Total COGS</td><td>$ 25,955.78</td></tr>
<tr><td>2</td><td>Gross Profit</td><td>$ 39,953.38</td></tr>
<tr><td>Expense</td><td></td><td></td></tr>
<tr><td></td><td>60100 - Automobile</td><td>$ 329.80</td></tr>
<tr><td></td><td>60600 - Bank Service Charges</td><td>$ 12.50</td></tr>
<tr><td></td><td>62100 - Insurance</td><td>$ 2,086.72</td></tr>
<tr><td></td><td>62400 - Interest Expense</td><td>$ 101.14</td></tr>
<tr><td></td><td>62700 - Payroll Expenses</td><td>$ 9,103.22</td></tr>
<tr><td></td><td>64200 - Repairs</td><td>$ -</td></tr>
<tr><td></td><td>64800 - Tools and Machinery</td><td>$ 25.00</td></tr>
<tr><td></td><td>65100 - Utilities</td><td>$ 121.53</td></tr>
<tr><td>3</td><td>Total Expense</td><td>$ 11,779.91</td></tr>
<tr><td></td><td>Net Ordinary Income</td><td>$ 28,173.47</td></tr>
<tr><td>4</td><td>Net Income</td><td>$ 28,173.47</td></tr>
</table>

Your Power Numbers:
1. Total Income
2. Gross Profit
3. Total Expenses
4. Net Income

Use Your Power Numbers to Create Predictable Profits by calculating the following items:

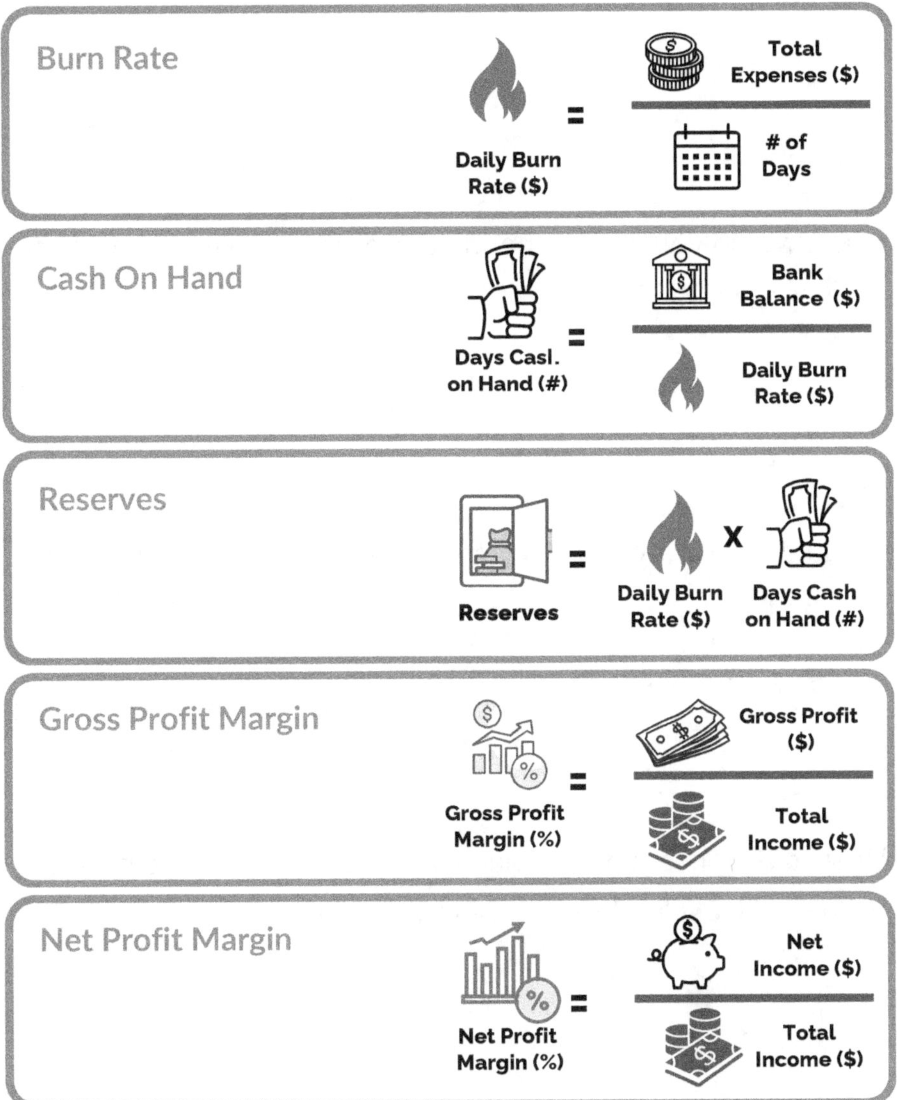

Refer back to the book *First This, Then That* to make some strategic plans about these numbers.

Budget Thoughts

How is having a budget in your business helpful?

What would you like to spend your profit on? How can you start saving for that now?

If you did no more work from today on, when would you run out of money?

What difference would a plan that helps you manage profits, reserves and cash flow make for your business?

Notes

Notes

Chapter 4

Business Model Roadmap
Creating Your Profitable Path

Circle the revenue model you use in your business.

4 Revenue Models

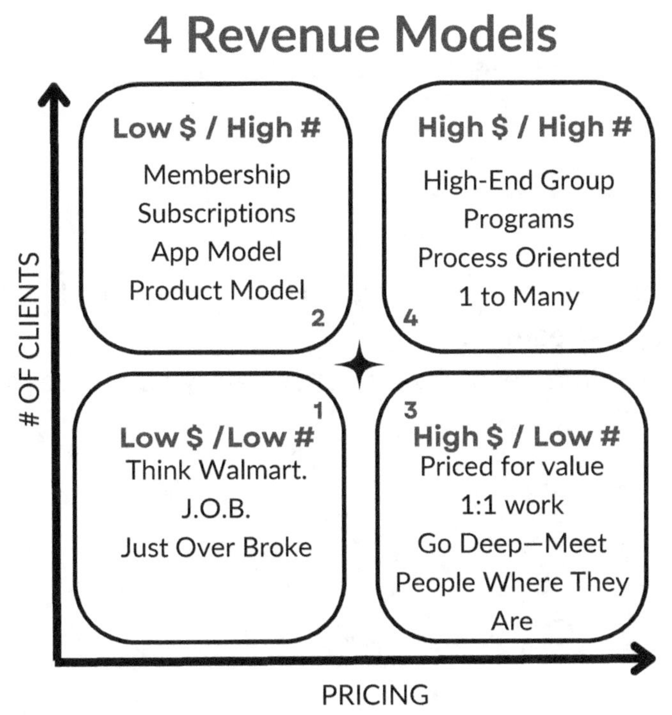

Adding on Additional Revenue Streams?

Is that the correct revenue model? Why or why not? Evaluate its strengths and weaknesses and consider if it's the best fit for your business goals.

How do you feel about your current revenue streams? Do you feel like there's potential for more, but something's holding you back?

What challenges are you facing when it comes to adding a new revenue stream?
Is it a lack of time, resources, or uncertainty about where to start?

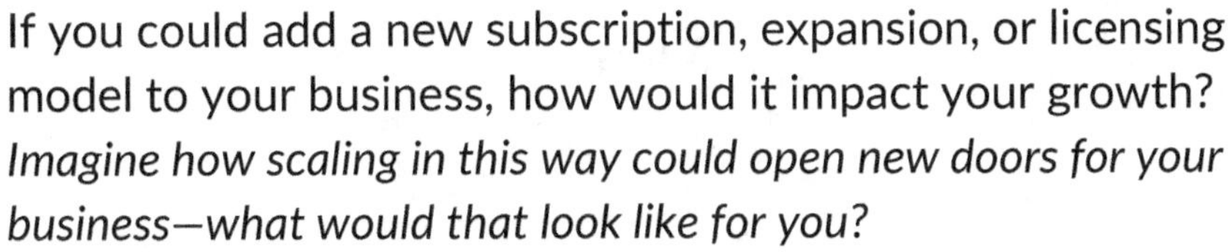

If you could add a new subscription, expansion, or licensing model to your business, how would it impact your growth? *Imagine how scaling in this way could open new doors for your business—what would that look like for you?*

What's been stopping you from exploring these opportunities? *Are you feeling overwhelmed by the idea, or do you need more guidance on where to begin?*

How would it feel to know you've laid the groundwork to confidently expand your business when the time is right? *How could you start planning now to be ready when the opportunity arises?*

Notes

Notes

Notes

Chapter 5

Winning Customers
Crafting Value Propositions
That Drive Conversions

Step 1: Defining Your Value

How clearly can you identify three functional reasons clients buy from you (e.g., efficiency, durability, cost savings)?

    ☐ Very clear

    ☐ Somewhat clear

    ☐ Unclear

How confident are you in identifying three emotional reasons clients are drawn to your business (e.g., trust, brand connection)?

    ☐ Very confident

    ☐ Somewhat confident

    ☐ Not confident

Can you clearly define three reasons your clients buy from you based on Esteem, Recognition, Achievement, or Impact (Maslow's highest needs)?

    ☐ Yes, I can

    ☐ I struggle with this

    ☐ I haven't considered this before

How easily can you narrow your top reasons for buying down to four core reasons?

- ☐ Very easily
- ☐ Somewhat easily
- ☐ It's challenging

How well do you understand why your top clients chose your business?

- ☐ Very well
- ☐ Somewhat well
- ☐ I'm not sure

Step 2: Identifying Your Client's Journey

How clearly can you define the main problem your business solves for clients?

- ☐ Very clear
- ☐ Somewhat clear
- ☐ Unclear

How well do you understand the impact or pain your clients feel from not solving this problem?

- ☐ I understand it deeply
- ☐ I have a general understanding
- ☐ I need to explore this more

How clearly can you describe the benefits and emotional payoff your clients experience after solving their problem?

- ☐ Very clear
- ☐ Somewhat clear
- ☐ Unclear

Step 3: Delivering Your Value

How confident are you in articulating how your services or products serve your clients (without listing every task)?

    ☐ Very confident

    ☐ Somewhat confident

    ☐ Not confident

Do you feel clients understand the key outcomes they'll achieve by working with you?

    ☐ Yes, they do

    ☐ I'm not sure

    ☐ No, I need to clarify this

Step 4: Crafting Your "Yes" Formula

How well can you explain your Relevance—how you solve problems and the direct benefits of choosing you?

    ☐ I can explain it well

    ☐ I struggle with it

    ☐ I need help defining it

How clearly can you define your Differentiation—what makes you stand out from competitors?

    ☐ Very clear

    ☐ Somewhat clear

    ☐ Unclear

How confident are you in expressing your Client Value Proposition (CVP) in a single statement?

    ☐ Very confident

    ☐ Somewhat confident

    ☐ Not confident

Notes

Notes

Notes

Chapter 6

Turning Ideas Into Reality
Key Steps to Business Feasibility

1. Key Resources: *Evaluating What You Have vs. What You Need*

How confident are you that you have the necessary resources (investment, IT, personnel, time, etc.) to bring your business idea to life?
- ☐ Very confident
- ☐ Somewhat confident
- ☐ Not confident at all

Which of the following resource areas do you already have covered? (Check all that apply)
- ☐ Financial investment
- ☐ IT infrastructure
- ☐ Key personnel
- ☐ Compliance and legal
- ☐ Systems and processes
- ☐ External partners or vendors
- ☐ Other (explain)

For the resources you still need, what are your next steps to acquire them?

2. Key Activities: *Understanding Your Critical Business Operations*
Rank the importance of the following activities in your business
(1 = least important, 5 = most important):

1 2 3 4 5 Production

1 2 3 4 5 Marketing

1 2 3 4 5 Sales

1 2 3 4 5 Customer service

1 2 3 4 5 Other (please specify):

1 2 3 4 5 Other (please specify):

How clearly do you understand the key steps required to execute the above items successfully?
- ☐ I have a clear plan in place
- ☐ I have a general idea but need more details
- ☐ I'm unclear on how to move forward

What's one high-level process you know needs more attention to ensure your business delivers on its value proposition?

3. Key Partners: Leveraging Your Network

How strong is your current network in helping you achieve your business goals?

- ☐ Very strong—multiple partners ready to assist
- ☐ Somewhat strong—I have a few key partners
- ☐ Weak—I need to expand my network

Who do you consider your top three key partners or potential partners?

What gaps do you need to fill in terms of partnerships or external resources?

Notes

Notes

Notes

Chapter 7

Profitable Pricing
Strategies for Sustainable Growth

Reflecting on Your Unique Value
Remember: If you can clearly communicate your unique distinction, then truly, you have no competition.

How do you feel about the unique benefits you're providing? *Do you believe these benefits set you apart from competitors, or is there something holding you back from fully communicating your distinction?*

How is your product or service enhancing the lives of your customers? *Can you confidently see the impact, or are you unsure how to measure it?*

What makes your services or products superior to those of your competitors? *How well do you understand these advantages, and are you effectively showcasing them?*

Does your pricing reflect the value you give your customers? *If not, what's stopping you from pricing in line with the true worth of your offering?*

Evaluating Your Costs and Growth Potential
How well do you manage your business expenses while pursuing growth?
   □ I'm fully on top of it
   □ I'm managing, but there's room for improvement
   □ I feel overwhelmed by my expenses

How aligned are your profitability targets with your growth goals?
   □ Completely aligned
   □ Somewhat aligned
   □ Not aligned at all

What are your growth plans for the business, and how excited are you about the future?

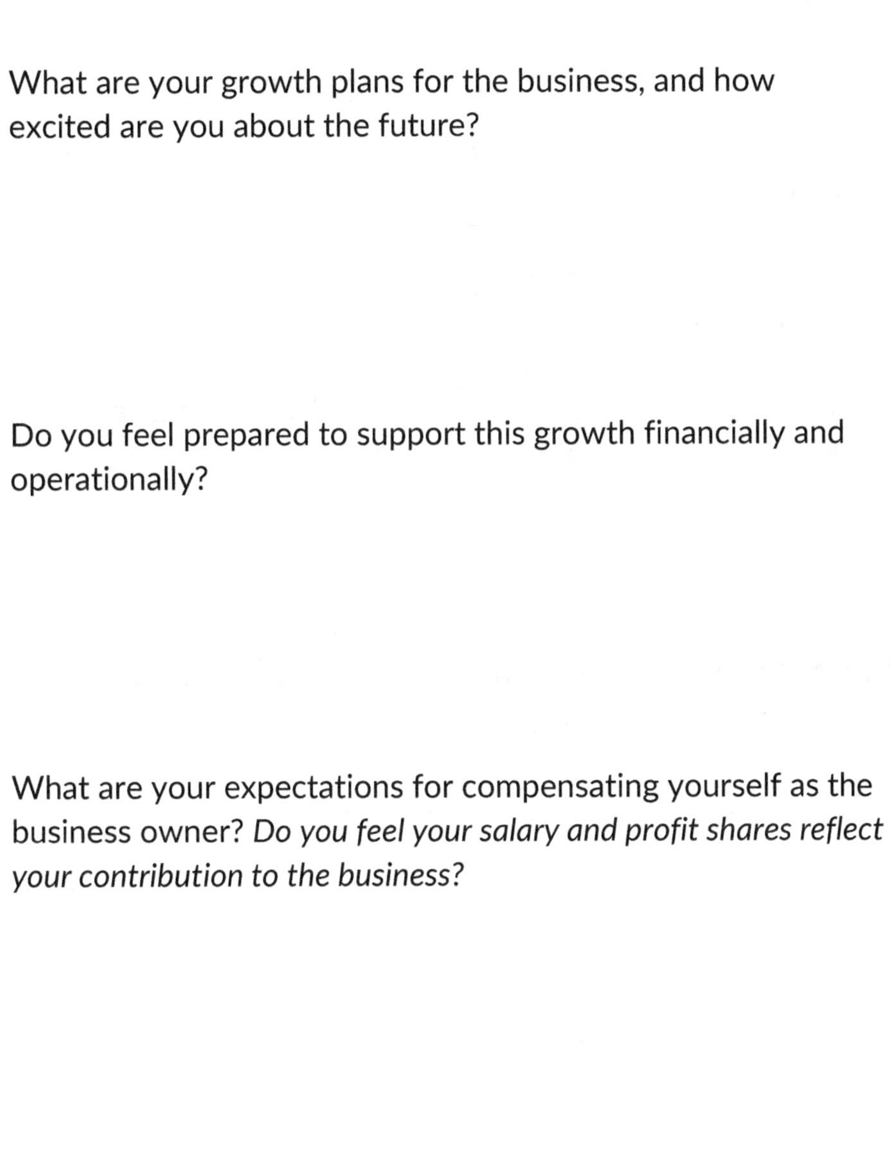

43

Do you feel prepared to support this growth financially and operationally?

What are your expectations for compensating yourself as the business owner? *Do you feel your salary and profit shares reflect your contribution to the business?*

Finding Balance In Operations

How sustainable are your current work hours for long-term growth?
- □ Completely sustainable
- □ Somewhat sustainable
- □ Not sustainable

How confident are you in your team's ability to manage capacity and meet your revenue goals?
- □ Very confident
- □ Somewhat confident
- □ Not confident

What expectations do you have for your team's capacity and how that ties to revenue generation?

What adjustments need to be made to ensure and protect profitability in the business?

Assessing Your Time and Compensation

Do you feel your compensation as an owner reflects the value you bring to the business?
    ☐ Yes, I'm fairly compensated
    ☐ I could be compensated more
    ☐ No, I'm under-compensated

Are you effectively delegating tasks that could be handled by others?
    ☐ Yes, I delegate appropriately
    ☐ Somewhat, but I could improve
    ☐ No, I do too much myself

What tasks are you currently handling that could be delegated to someone with a lower hourly rate?

What's stopping you from delegating these responsibilities?

How does your current pricing compare to your effective hourly rate? *Does it feel right, or is there a gap between what you're charging and the effort you're putting in?*

When you compare your effective rate with your pricing, what did you discover that you didn't know before? *How do you feel about making adjustments to reflect your true value?*

Notes

Notes

Chapter 8

Making Changes Stick
Proven Methods for
Sustainable Business Transformation

Mindset Shifts: Turning Fear into Fuel for Positive Change
Most people fear change. It's a natural reaction. List out all the significant changes in your life and put a smiley face next to the ones you view as positive and a frown face next to the ones you see as negative.

What do you notice from this exercise?

How many of the positive changes were initiated by your choice?

How many of the negative changes were outside of your control?

As you are considering changes in your business, what do you need to keep in mind?

Notes

Notes

Chapter 9

Transforming Your Business
Marketing, Operations, and Pricing

Step 1: Identify Your High-Value Categories

Everyone places value on different aspects of a business. Identify the three key categories where you personally place high value in your business (e.g., customer service, product quality, innovation). Note: These will guide your decisions in marketing, operations, and pricing.

Write down your top three categories of value:

1.

2.

3.

Think about why each category is important to you and how it reflects your business. How are these priorities mirrored in your current practices?

Step 2: One Small Change

Identify one small change you can implement in your business (e.g., adjusting your marketing strategy, refining your pricing). Write down the specific change:

List three ways this change will improve your business:

1.

2.

3.

Create a brief action plan for implementing the change:
What resources will you need?

Who will be responsible for overseeing this change?

What timeline will you set for completion?

Step 3: Preparing Your Team for the Transition

What message will you share with your team about the upcoming change?

List potential concerns your team may have and how you plan to address them.
Concern 1:
How you will address it?

Concern 2:
How you will address it?

Concern 3:
How you will address it?

What steps can you take to involve your team in decision-making?

How will you encourage feedback and collaboration from your team?

Step 4: Implementation and Flexibility

Assign roles and responsibilities for implementation:
Who will lead the execution of this change?

Who will monitor progress?

Who else needs to be involved?

Prepare to track to know if progress is good or not:
List key metrics or milestones you will track to ensure
progress:

Prepare for flexibility:
What potential roadblocks might you face?

How will you remain flexible if things don't go as planned?

Step 5: Post-Change Review: Tracking Progress and Success

It's important to regularly review the results of any change you implement.

What is the date you will review the outcomes of your change?

Schedule a meeting with your team to evaluate the progress. It can be the same date as you review the outcomes or a different date within a week or so. What date will that be?

During the meeting, focus on the following topics:
- Review what has changed and what progress has been made.
- Discuss feedback from the team on the results.
- Identify any adjustments that need to be made to improve the outcome.
- Celebrate small successes to reinforce positive momentum.

Final Notes: Embrace Incremental Change

The key to sustainable transformation is not overhauling your business overnight but making small, strategic adjustments over time. Write down any final reflections or notes on how you can apply this mindset moving forward.

Notes

Notes

Chapter 10

Mastering Growth Momentum
Strategic Foundations
for Predictable Returns

Think about a recent time when your business experienced a surge in growth.

What initiated it?

How did you and your team respond?

Think about the momentum of the growth, were you able to sustain that growth, or did it taper off?

What lessons were learned that can shape growth for the future in the business?

Think deeply about the current strategies in your business. Are your strategies mostly reactive or proactive?

Why would it matter if your strategies are reactive or proactive?

What do you need to change in your business because of these thoughts? (Remember that the past 2 chapters discuss how to implement needed change.)

Notes

Notes

Chapter 11

Growth GPS

Turning Data into Actionable Strategies

Calculate Your KPI's

Your money tells a story about your business. In order to understand the story, start by running the following KPIs for the last three years of your business.

	KPI's: 7 Metrics of Growth	2 Years Ago	Last Year	This Year
1	Leads (#)			
2	Conversion Rate	%	%	%
	—# of Clients—			
3	Average Sale Per Client	$	$	$
4	Average # of Purchases			
	—Gross Profit —	$	$	$
5	Gross Profit Margin	%	%	%
6	Lifetime Value of a Client	$	$	$
7	Cost of Client Acquisition	$	$	$

As you look at your numbers, what story do they tell? Remember to look in the *First This, Then That Book* for more information.

What changes need to occur? Where can you improve?

Notes

Notes

Chapter 12

Your Growth Mindset
Resilience Reimagined for Business Success

When have you ever had something totally unexpected disrupt your business? If so, what was it?

How did you recover? Did it give you a renewed sense of strength and resolve or did you feel defeated? Explain how you felt.

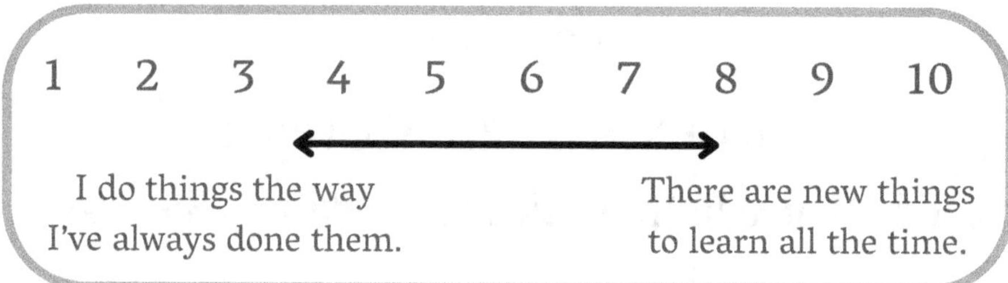

Doing things the way you have always done them is great for routine tasks. It is typically called a fixed mindset. Embracing change and new ways of doing things is typically called a growth mindset. As an entrepreneur, how can having a growth mindset serve you better?

Create a Personal Timeline of Your Entrepreneurial Journey

1. On the timeline below, mark significant moments of success.
2. Now go back and mark significant moments of failure.

   NOTE: Please do not use these bad moments in the past to give shame, blame, or guilt. You did the best you could in the past. Use your current reflections to have better moments in the future.

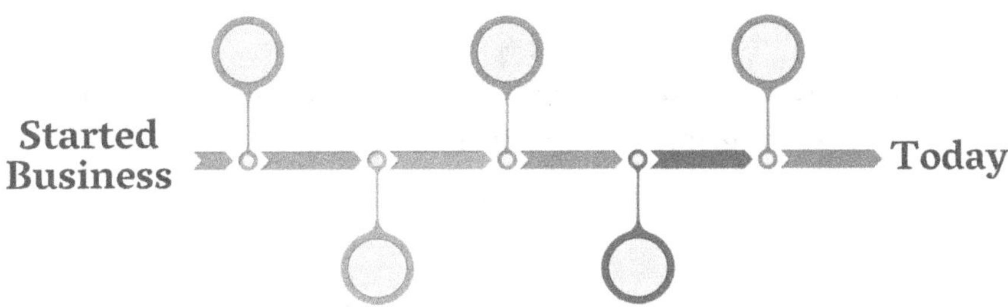

Reflect on these pivotal points, focusing on the "bounce-back" moments.
How did you feel at the time?

What strategies did you employ to overcome these challenges?

Consider what your current self would advise your past self, armed with hindsight and experience.

Again, please do not use these bad moments in the past to give shame, blame, or guilt. You did the best you could in the past. Use your current reflections to have better moments in the future.

Notes

Notes

Chapter 13

Level Up
Scaling Your Business for Maximum Profit

What period are you currently in Growth, Scalability, Recovery or Status Quo?

How do you know?

Does your current stage align with where you want to be? Why or why not?

What holds you back from reaching the next level in your business?

How well does your business align with your personal vision? If it does align, how does that strengthen you? If it does not align, how is that stopping you?

Notes

Notes

If You Liked This Book ...

In our next book, ***Scaling Rich™: Creating Predictable Profits to Grow Your Business without Burnout***, we share how to scale your business efficiently and profitably while upholding your core values.

Scaling Rich is crafted to resonate with every entrepreneur. It details Josh's journey as he scales his business without compromising what's important to him.

Imagine running a business where everything operates smoothly, your team is thriving, and every decision enhances the company along with your most valued relationships and experiences. In *Scaling Rich*, you'll learn to pinpoint the perfect moment to shift from growth to scaling, maximize your profits, and improve cash flow, stepping up as a visionary leader who transcends daily tasks.

Scaling Rich introduces a fresh perspective on growth beyond boosting revenue or market share. It's about creating a business that succeeds financially and enriches your personal life, offering a sustainable alternative to the relentless hustle culture. It aligns your business ambitions with your personal values and life goals.

You'll uncover advanced strategies to enhance your operational efficiency and profitability, apply savvy financial tactics to fund your growth, and intelligently invest in ways that further your company's goals. These strategies lay the groundwork for a business that serves your ambitions and supports the life you love.

Get ready to transform your business and personal life approach with *Scaling Rich*. This book provides a comprehensive blueprint for achieving prosperity and enriching the relationships and experiences that mean the most to you.

WHEN YOU ARE READY,
WE ARE HERE TO HELP YOU.

About Your Biz Rules

At Your Biz Rules, we help business owners grow with clarity, focus, and action. Our *First This, Then That* approach is designed to guide you step-by-step through sustainable business growth. We know that growth isn't about doing more —it's about doing the right things at the right time.

How We Help

Profitable Growth Incubator - 6-month cohort that helps you prioritize, take action, and build momentum in real-time.

Fractional CFO Services - Financial guidance for long-term business profitability and growth.

Business Audits - Uncover hidden opportunities and inefficiencies to help you scale faster.

Private Consulting - One-on-one support to tackle your toughest business challenges.

Workshops & Training - Equip your team with actionable business strategies.

Speaking - Interactive and engaging topics that will have your audience asking for more.

Ready to get started? To learn more about how we can help you scale your business profitably and successfully, contact us at https://yourbizrules.com/chat.

 www.yourbizrules.com

 support@yourbizrules.com

About The Author

Leslie Hassler is a dynamic author, speaker, business strategist, and founder of Your Biz Rules. Leslie empowers entrepreneurs to cultivate strategies that lead to sustainable growth and increased profitability while avoiding burnout.

With a proven track record in business, finance, mindset, marketing, and entrepreneurship, Leslie's holistic approach has helped businesses across all industries overcome challenges and thrive in a balanced manner.

Many business owners who are experts in their field come to Leslie and Your Biz Rules after some measure of success to understand how to run a business that meets their business and their life goals.

Leslie shares her expertise in her books *First This, Then That* and *Scaling Rich*. She has been recognized on stages across the United States, including prestigious events such as the National Association of Women Business Owners and the Women's Business Enterprise National Council. Her insights have also been featured in notable publications like Entrepreneur.com.

Leslie is a mother of two, avid traveler, Past President of NAWBO DFW, and alumni of the Goldman Sachs 10K Small Business program. Your Biz Rules is WBENC, HUB, and AI Mastery Certified.

www.ingramcontent.com/pod-product-compliance
Lightning Source LLC
Chambersburg PA
CBHW061346140726
47997CB00003B/1075